The Angel of the Prairies
Or
A Dream of the Future

By Parley Parker Pratt

ISBN: 978-1-63118-541-0

Mormon History
Series

Other Books in this Series and Related Titles

Pearl of Great Price by Joseph Smith (978-1-63118-539-7)

The Book of Abraham: Mormon History by George Reynolds (978-1-63118-540-3)

The Testament of Abraham by Abraham (978-1-63118-441-3)

The Book of Parables by Enoch (978-1-63118-429-1)

The Secrets of Enoch by Enoch (978-1-63118-449-9)

American Indian Freemasonry by A C Parker (978-1-63118-460-4)

Lost Chapters of the Book of Daniel and Related Writings (978-1-63118-417-8)

The Book of the Watchers by Enoch (978-1-63118-416-1)

Book of Dreams by Enoch (978-1-63118-437-6)

The Hymns of Hermes by G. R. S. Mead (978-1-63118-405-5)

The Book of Astronomical Secrets by Enoch (978-1-63118-443-7)

The Two Great Pillars of Boaz and Jachin by A Mackey &c (978-1-63118-433-8)

The Regius Poem or Halliwell Manuscript by King Solomon (978-1-63118-447-5)

The Lost Keys of Freemasonry or The Secret of Hiram Abiff (978-1-63118-427-7)

Brothers & Builders by Joseph Fort Newton (978-1-63118-506-9)

Symbolism and Discourses on the Entered Apprentice, Fellowcraft and Master Mason Blue Lodge Degrees by various (978-1-63118-413-0)

Freemasonry, Mithraism and the Ancient Mysteries by various (978-1-63118-407-9)

The Ceremony of Initiation: Analysis & Commentary (978-1-63118-473-4)

The Symbols and Legends of Masonry by C H Vail (978-1-63118-504-5)

The Janeites, The Man Who Would Be King and Other Stories of Freemasonry by Rudyard Kipling (978-1-63118-480-2)

Audio Versions are also available on Audible, Amazon and Apple

Other Books in this Series and Related Titles

The Hidden Mysteries of Christianity by Annie Besant (978–1–63118–534–2)

Rosicrucian Rules, Secret Signs, Codes and Symbols by various (978-1-63118-488-8)

History and Teachings of the Rosicrucians by W W Westcott &c (978-1-63118-487-1)

Freemasonry and the Egyptian Mysteries by C. W. Leadbeater (978-1-63118-456-7)

The Sepher Yetzirah and the Qabalah by M P Hall (978-1-63118-481-9)

The Psalms of Solomon by King Solomon (978-1-63118-439-0)

The Historic, Mythic and Mystic Christ by Annie Besant (978–1–63118–533–5)

Masonic and Rosicrucian History by M P Hall & H Voorhis (978-1-63118-486-4)

The Kabbalah of Masonry & Related Writings by E Levi &c (978-1-63118-453-6)

Some Deeper Aspects of Masonic Symbolism by A E Waite (978-1-63118-461-1)

Masonic Symbolism of King Solomon's Temple by A Mackey &c (978-1-63118-442-0)

The Old Past Master by Carl H Claudy (978-1-63118-464-2)

The Influence of Pythagoras on Freemasonry and Other Essays (978-1-63118-404-8)

The Mysteries of Freemasonry & the Druids by various (978-1-63118-444-4)

Masonic Symbolism of the Apron & the Altar by various (978-1-63118-428-4)

The Book of Wisdom of Solomon by King Solomon (978-1-63118-502-1)

Masonic Symbolism of Easter and the Christ in Masonry (978-1-63118-434-5)

The Odes of Solomon by King Solomon (978-1-63118-503-8)

Ancient Mysteries and Secret Societies by M P Hall (978-1-63118-410-9)

The Golden Verses of Pythagoras: Five Translations (978-1-63118-479-6)

Freemasonry & Catholicism by Max Heindel (978-1-63118-508-3)

A Few Masonic Sermons by A. C. Ward &c (978-1-63118-435-2)

Audio versions are also available on Audible, Amazon and Apple

Table of Contents

THE
ANGEL OF THE PRAIRIES;
A DREAM OF THE FUTURE,

BY
ELDER PARLEY PARKER PRATT,

One of the Twelve Apostles of the Church of Jesus Christ of
Latter-day Saints.

A. PRATT, PUBLISHER.
SALT LAKE CITY, UTAH:

DESERET NEWS PRINTING AND PUBLISHING
ESTABLISHMENT.

1880

PREFACE

THE thrilling and interesting narrative contained in this little book, though setting up no claim to being an authentic or infallible prophecy, yet probably contains as much condensed truth and as little fiction as any work in any age, that has inspired truth for its foundation, and romance simply for its embellishment and adornings.

This manuscript was read in Nauvoo, in a Council of the Church, in the presence of the Prophet Joseph Smith, but never appeared in print until last Spring, in the Northern Light, when it became at once the admiration of all the Saints who had the privilege of its perusal.

While purporting to be written under the similitude of a dream or vision, we will state that no such dream or vision was had by the writer, the whole manuscript having been written at Nauvoo, in the Winter of 1843-4.

The useful and elevating object of the author shines in every page of the work, and not a hurtful feature can be found in it. As will be seen, the book contains twenty pages of reading matter,--twice the amount we supposed it to contain--we shall therefore be under the necessity of charging twenty-five cents a copy, instead of fifteen cents.

ABINADI PRATT,
PUBLISHER.
Salt Lake City, January, 1880.

THE ANGEL OF THE PRAIRIES
or
A DREAM OF THE FUTURE

BEING a native of a small and retired village of New England, and trained to the strictest habits of industry, I had grown to manhood without seeing much of the world, having never traveled to exceed twenty miles from home. As is not unfrequently the case with New Englanders, my ideas were severe extremely limited and narrow in regard to the extent and resources of the West. I had heard of prairies, to be sure, or open untimbered fields, but could form no other idea of them than to compare them to some of our marshes, which were by nature destitute of timber because they were too low and wet to produce it.

I know not how or why it was the case, but for some reason I had been, from my earliest remembrance, impressed with a longing desire and a fixed determination to visit and to explore the mighty, the mysterious West. To this inclination my friends were always opposed. They would often reason as follows: "Have you not a quiet home in the midst of friends, peace and plenty? Have you not a sufficiency of wealth and of all things which are calculated to make you contented and happy? Why then will you go to the West. Why will you tear yourself from all these blessings and from society, and wander through uncultivated forests and amid dangers, toils and sufferings, amid the hiss of serpents, the howl of wild beasts, and the whoops and yells of men more savage than they? To these expostulations I could never give a satisfactory answer, but still I wanted to go.

At the age of twenty-one, being free, and in possession of ready money sufficient to place me beyond the reach of immediate want, I resolved to break through every restraint and to gratify my thirst for travel. I took leave of my friends with many tears and blessings on their part, and with feelings deep and indescribable on my own. I soon had the gratification of beholding Niagara Falls, the great lakes and dense forests of the West, as well as the splendid towns, the domestic villas and the delightful fields, interspersed here and there, amid the wild and romantic scenes of nature. But these indulgences only served to increase my desire for still further research. I soon penetrated farther into the interior, where for the first time a grand prairie scenery opened before me. This exceeded all the western wonders I had before seen. After traveling for some hours over a gently undulating landscape, smooth and beautiful as a village park, and covered with grass and flowers, extending on all sides as far as the eye could reach, I ascended a gradually rising eminence, and halted to look around me. All seemed like a splendid vision passing all reality, and putting imagination at defiance to imitate. A green field of grass and flowers extended on all sides as far as the eye could reach; without a horse or tree, a man or animal, to intercept the sight or break upon the lonely and sublime repose which reigned around me. The landscape was sufficiently diversified in hills and valleys and other gentle elevations, neither presenting the dull monotony of a level plain, nor the rough and abrupt appearance of hills too steep for easy cultivation. Indeed, an English nobleman would have found a pleasant passage for a coach and six in any direction from where I stood. The soil was vastly rich and the surface was smooth and even, the whole landscape resembling a boundless field of green wheat interspersed with lilies and sunflowers. With one glance of the eye, I beheld an extent of country sufficient for the home of happy millions. "Here," thought I, "within the reach of my natural vision, might exist an empire more extensive, numerous and wealthy, than some of the most renowned kingdoms of the old world! And yet not one human being possesses the knowledge, courage and ambition to claim it as his own possession. Nay, they would rather seek a precarious subsistence in the streets of some overgrown and populous town, or kill and conquer the inhabitants of some miserable country already overpeopled."

While indulging in this strange reverie--one thought gave rise to another--my narrow heart enlarged and I began to extend my inquiries as to the real boundaries of these mighty and extended fields and their future destiny. I naturally concluded that so fine a country and such vast riches would not always be overlooked by the enterprising and industrious. That immigration would come rolling on in its westward tendency, and with it the march of empire, till these lonely plains would be all peopled and these rich resources made to yield support to happy millions.

With these thoughts still deeply working in my mind, I pursued my journey, and at the close of day arrived at an humble cottage where, with an appetite sharpened by fatigue, I partook of such simple refreshments as the place afforded, and retired to rest, my mind still filled with thoughts more sublimely great, grand and solemn than had ever before occupied my bosom. A deep and unquiet slumber soon came over me, and my mind was carried away in a most extraordinary vision. A messenger of a mild and intelligent countenance, suddenly stood before me, arrayed in robes of dazzling splendor. "Fear not," said he, "thou son of mortal! For I am the Angel of the Prairies. I hold the keys of the mysteries of this wonderful country, to me is committed the fate of empires and the destiny of nations. Come then, with me, and I will show thee the secret purposes of fate in relation to this, the most extraordinary of all countries!"

Overjoyed with the information, and gathering confidence from the kind and generous appearance of the messenger, I arose and accompanied him. We were wafted through the air at a rapid rate, for some hundreds of miles, in a western direction, a little bearing to the south. At length we came to a halt in an elevated green and flowery plain on the southern bank of the Missouri river--not far from the line that divides the Indian Territory from the States--a place of surpassing beauty and loveliness.

"Young man," said the Angel of the Prairies, "take this glass and look around thee." He then handed me a curious glass by which I was enabled to view the entire country from sea to sea. Looking to the north, I beheld the extensive and fertile plains of Iowa and Wisconsin, composed chiefly of rich, rolling prairies, interspersed with beautiful groves of timber, and watered with numerous streams, some of which were navigable for hundreds of miles; and others forming numerous and valuable water powers for the propelling of mills and machinery. These fertile and flowery plains and groves extended for many hundreds of miles to the north, and were finally terminated by large and extensive forests of pine, which could easily be rafted down the currents of the numerous streams, and be used in the erection of buildings, towns and cities, throughout the whole extent of the unlimited prairies. The central portion of these vast territories abounded in rich ores, such as lead, iron and coal; and the northern portions abounded in copper. The vegetable, mineral and commercial resources of these territories seemed capable of sustaining and employing one hundred millions of people, while at present they contained hardly as many thousands.

Turning from these, I looked eastward, where the states of Missouri, Arkansas and Illinois presented a vast territory of some five hundred miles in extent, similar in fertility and resources to the territories above described, consisting of rich, beautiful and fertile prairies, mingled with delightful groves of timber, and penetrated with numerous large and expansive rivers, on the bosom of which might float the commerce of nations and empires. These states were calculated to sustain at least another hundred millions of souls, although at present not occupied by one million.

After viewing with wonder and delight these beautiful states, I cast my eyes toward the south and southwest. The vision now lengthened in the distance, and some thousands of miles of country expanded to my view, including the vast plains, and fertile forests and vales of Texas and Mexico; still presenting a vast quantity of unlimited meadows and prairies, rich and beautiful as Eden, and abounding in vegetable and mineral wealth. These countries were abundantly sufficient to sustain two hundred millions more of inhabitants, although at present possessing a population of less than ten millions.

Having contemplated the green fields, the flowery plains, the dense forests and towering mountains of this vast country till lost and overwhelmed in astonishment, I turned to the west. Here I beheld a tract of country lately surveyed and appropriated for the location of the Indian tribes. It was bounded on the east by the states of Missouri and Arkansas, on the south by Texas, on the west by the Great American Desert and on the north by the almost unexplored and inhospitable regions of Canada, or more properly by the Missouri river, embracing some six hundred miles from north to south, and some two hundred from east to west. This, like the countries before described, abounded in alternate rich, rolling prairies and woodlands, capable for sustaining a population of at least fifty millions; although at present peopled with a few Indian tribes consisting of less than half a million. "Young man," said the Angel of the Prairies, "you have now beheld the great meadows of the West, an almost unbroken and continuous field of prairie, bounded on the east by the Wabash and Lake Michigan, on the north by the prairies of Wisconsin and Iowa, on the west by the Great Desert, and on the south by Central America, and averaging some three thousand miles long and some seven hundred broad; being mostly a rich and fertile plain, watered like Eden, and more productive than the plains of Euphrates. Its people are at present few, but its resources are immense, and it is abundantly calculated to sustain at least one half of the present population of the globe. You now stand in a central position, in the midst of the great American continent. Here is the spot which is destined for the seat of empire, and here shall the ambassadors of all nations resort with a tribute of homage to a greater than Cyrus.

"The seat of empire," continued he, "began in the eastern Eden, but its progress has always been westward. It lighted on the plains of Euphrates, where, under Nimrod, Nebuchadnezzar, Cyrus, Alexander and others, it rested for a time. But, migrating still westward, it took its seat in Palestine, and finally on the banks of the Nile, from whence it passed to Rome in Italy, where it swayed a long and bloody sceptre, and in course of time penetrated to the western islands of Europe, where it sojourned for a time as if to prepare for a voyage. Holding still its sea-girt throne, it sent out a forlorn hope, a kind of advance guard to prepare its way in the wilderness. These parsed over the great waters and finally strengthened themselves until they founded a seat of government on the extreme eastern shore of this vast continent. This was in the infancy of the American Republic, quite central and convenient. On this account some narrow minded mortals, taking only a momentary view of the subject, supposed that the seat of empire, after progressing for thousands of years, had now found a resting place where it would tarry forever. Poor mistaken mortals, how little did they know of the country they were in, and how much less of the decrees of infinite wisdom!"

These words being ended, the Angel of the Prairies bade me tarry awhile on this second spot, and he would then return and unfold to me the mysteries of the future, and the hitherto secret and impenetrable decrees of fate. With this charge he vanished from my sight. A mist of darkness suddenly overspread the landscape--a veil of oblivion enshrouded me round, and the whole scene was shut from my view. Indistinct shadows and confused forms occupied my imagination and troubled my slumbers, and finally a long time seemed to pass away without any distinct recollection of events. Suddenly a hand touched me, and a voice exclaimed, "Mortal, awake! The Angel of the Prairie, has returned, and the time is fulfilled. Arise! Stand up-right, and look around thee." At the voice of his words I seemed to awake as from a deep sleep, the darkness dispersed, and light ineffable shone around me. I found myself in the same central position where he had left me, and which he had pointed out as the final seat of empire. But oh! how changed!

Instead of a flowery plain without inhabitants, I beheld an immense city, extending on all sides and thronged with myriad's of people, apparently of all nations. In the midst of this city stood a magnificent temple, which, in magnitude and splendor, exceeded everything of the kind before known upon the earth. Its foundations were of precious stones; its walls like polished gold; its windows of agates, clear as crystal; and its roof of a dazzling brightness, its top, like the lofty Andes, seemed to mingle with the skies; while a bright cloud overshadowed it, from which extended rays of glory and brightness in all the magnificent colors of the rainbow. The whole buildings thereof seemed to cover some eight or ten acres of ground. "This," said the Angel of the Prairies, "is the sanctuary of freedom, the palace of the great King, and the center of a universal government. Follow me and you shall behold the magnificence, order and glory of His kingdom." So saying, we walked together to the gates of the temple. These were twelve in number; three on each side, and all standing open. Numerous parties and servants were in waiting, and guides and instructors were busy in attendance on strangers, who were passing to and from the temple, with an air of confident freedom, and clad in mingled and varied costumes of all nations.

By a secret watchword from the Angel to the porter or keeper of the gate, we were permitted to pass the eastern centre gate into the court yard. This was a large square surrounding the temple, and containing a square mile of land, enclosed with a strong wall of masonry, and ornamented with walks, grass plots, flowers and shady groves of ornamental trees, the whole arranged in the most perfect taste, and with an elegance, neatness and beauty, that might well compare with Eden. Here the eye was dazzled with scenes of beauty, the ear saluted with innumerable strains of music from birds of varied notes and plumage. And here the balmy breath of morn seemed perfumed with sweets more delicious than the spicy groves of Arabia. Here, in short, the entire senses seemed overwhelmed with enjoyment and pleasure indescribable. Passing along a spacious walk, in the midst of scenes like these, he came to the eastern door of the temple, over which was inscribed, in letters of gold, the following:

"Here wisdom, knowledge and truth are blended!
Here mercy reigns and war is ended!
Here on these grounds all nations enter;
But here a tyrant dare not venture!"

On entering the outer court, we found ourselves in a large and splendid room, inside of which were doors opening in every direction, over which were inscribed the particular uses for which they were occupied. This outer court was ornamented and finished with monuments, paintings, maps, charts, engravings, etc., all of which were not only ornamental but highly instructive, and calculated to impart a world of information on astronomy, geography, history, geometry, theology, etc., etc. Among these, my attention was drawn to a large painting which represented huge piles of broken iron, and antique weapons of every description, heaped up together in the greatest confusion, from the ancient bow of steel, or the wooden bow and arrow and war club of the savage, to the most polished and renowned implements of modern warfare. All these were laid aside as useless, and men were represented in the act of beating swords into ploughshares and spears into pruning hooks.

"These," said the Angel of the Prairies, "are the implements of murder and cruelty with which poor, ignorant, mistaken mortals once made war upon each other; but they have long since been laid aside as useless, and the arts of war are no lodger studied or practiced on the earth." After viewing these things, my guide conducted me to a door, which opened into the inner course, and over which was written as follows:

"Within is freedom's throne exalted high!
Where, crowned with light and truth and majesty,
A royal host in robes of bright array,
Their peaceful sceptre o'er else nations sway."

On entering this room, a vast and extensive hall was opened before me, the walls of which were white and ornamented with various figures which I did not understand. In the midst of this hall was a vast throne as white as ivory, and ascended by seventy steps, and on either side the throne and of the steps leading to it, there were seats rising one above another. On this throne was seated an aged, venerable looking man. His hair was white, with age, and his countenance beamed with intelligence and affection indescribable, as if he were the father of the kingdoms and people over which he reigned. He was clad in robes of dazzling whiteness, while a glorious crown rested upon his brow; and a pillar of light above his head, seemed to diffuse over the whole scene a brilliance of glory and grandeur indescribable. There was something in his countenance which seemed to indicate that he had passed long years of struggle and exertion in the achievement of some mighty revolution, and been a man of sorrows and acquainted with grief. But, like the evening sun after a day of clouds and tempest, he seemed to smile with a dignity of repose. In connection with this venerable personage sat two others scarcely less venerable, and clad and crowned in the same manner. On the next seat below were twelve personages, much of the same appearance and clad in the same manner, with crowns upon their heads; while the descending seats were filled with some thousands of noble and dignified personages, all enrobed in white and crowned with authority, power and majesty, as kings and priests presiding among the sons of God.

"You now behold," said the Angel of the Prairies, "The Grand Presiding Council organized in wisdom, and holding the keys of power to bear rule over all the earth in righteousness. And of the increase and glory of their kingdoms their shall be no end." As he spoke thus, bands of instrumental music filled the temple with melody indescribable, accompanied with human voices, both male and female, all chiming in perfect harmony in a hymn of triumph, the words of which I could only understand in part. But the concluding lines were repeated in swelling strains of joy. They were as followers:

"Tho' earth and its treasures should melt in the fire,
And the starlight of heaven wax dim and expire;
Tho' yon planets no longer revolve in their spheres,
The earth make its day, or its circuit of years;
Tho' the fountain of joy all its light shall withhold,
And the moons and Sabbaths shall cease to behold;
Yet firm and unshaken this throne shall remain,
And the heirs of Old Israel eternally reign."

As the music ceased, the Angel said:

"Son of mortal! ascend with me, and I will show you the country which we explored together at the first." At this instant a door was opened, which we entered, and commenced to ascend a flight of steps. These gradually ascended upwards through a long and winding passage, till at length we found ourselves on a pinnacle of the temple. The air was pure and mild, the sky was clear, and the vision expended far and wide on all sides, without an intervening object. My guide now handed me the same curious glass in which I had formerly viewed the country. But now how different, how wonderful the change of all things around me! Instead of lone prairies and wild and dreary forests, I now beheld one vast extent of populous country. Cities, towns, villages, houses, palaces, gardens, farms, fields, orchards, and vineyards extended in endless variety where once I beheld little else but loneliness and desolation.

"This," said the Angel of the Prairies, "is the country in which, one hundred years ago, you commenced to explore, in your journey to the west. Behold," continued he, "what truth and knowledge and perseverance can accomplish in a single century." To this I replied: "I am lost in wonder and amazement, and can hardly understand what I see. Who are these populous nations and tribes, who in happy myriads occupy the country immediately to the west, which was formerly occupied by savage hordes, but which now presents one vast scene of neatness, beauty, civilization and happiness? Have the Indian tribes, then, been entirely exterminated, and their country overrun by civilized nations?"

"Nay," said he, "these are still the Indians. A mysterious Providence preserved their remnants, and gathered and concentrated them into one peaceful nation. When they were first brought together from all parts of the continent, they numbered a population of about seven millions of ignorant, degraded people. But the light of truth dawned upon them, and with it came all the blessings of peace, plenty, civilization, cleanliness, and beauty, which you behold, and they constitute some thirty-five millions, and occupy all the country west of the Mississippi and bordering on the Rocky Mountains.

After viewing these beautiful settlements and hearing this interesting account of tribes and nations which I had been traditioned to believe could never be tamed, but were destined to perish from the earth, I turned toward the east and inquired after the great family of States which had once constituted the united Republic of E Pluribus Unum. These, I believed, were vastly more populous and wealthy than formerly. But they seemed no longer identified as States, with their former geographical boundaries and political forms of government. At this I was greatly astonished, as I had been early impressed with the idea of the future greatness and permanency of our national institutions. Turning to the guide, I inquired by what strange connection of events or by what mighty revolutions the American system had been dissolved, and its elements blended with this great central and universal government, which, notwithstanding my former prepossessions, I was constrained to acknowledge as far superior in excellence, glory and perfection to the former. To this inquiry the Angel of the Prairies replied as follows:

"The American system was indeed glorious in its beginning, and was founded by wise and good men, in opposition to long established abuses and oppressive systems of the Old World. But it had its weakenesses and imperfections. These were taken advantage of by wicked and conspiring men, who were unwisely placed at the head of government, and who, by a loose and corrupt administration, gradually undermined that beautiful structure. In their polluted hands justice faltered, truth fell to the ground, equity could not enter, and virtue fled into the wilderness. A blind, sectarianized and corrupt populace formed themselves into numerous mobs, overturned the laws, and put at defiance the administration thereof. These were either joined by the officers of Government or secretly winked at and encouraged by them, until the injured and persecuted friends of law and order, finding no protection or redress, were forced to abandon their country and its institutions, now no longer in force, and to retreat into the wilderness, with the loss of a vast amount of property and many valuable lives. These carried with them the spirit of liberty which seemed as a cement to form them into union, and thus was formed a nucleus around which rallied by decrees all the virtue and patriotism of the nation. Thus rallied and re-organized, the bold and daring sons of liberty were able to stand in their own defense, and to hurl defiance upon their former enemies. Thus the spirit of freedom had withdrawn from the mass and they were abandoned, like king Saul of old, to destruction. Divisions and contentions arose, and multiplied to that degree that they soon destroyed each other, deluged the country in blood, and thus ended the confederation under the title of E Pluribus Unum.

"The remnant who fled into the wilderness and rallied to the standard of liberty on the plains of the West, combining the wisdom of former experience with the light of truth which shone into their hearts from above, laid the foundation of their perfect form of government--this mighty empire of liberty which you now see, and the institutions of which you shall be more fully informed in due time. The wisdom, intelligence and peace which flowed from this centre soon served as an ensign to the nations abroad. This filled some with envy, others with admiration and delight. The good, the great, the noble, the generous and patriotic lovers of truth rallied from all nations, and joining the standard of freedom, were a constantly increasing strength to their near and perfect organization. While by the same means the old and corrupt institutions were proportionately weakened and abandoned. This soon stirred the envy and jealousy of old and corrupt popovers to that degree that they united in a general declaration of war against their young and more prosperous neighbors. These allied powers sent out an armament of five hundred ships of the line, and half a million of men. Their object was not only to gratify their vengeance and envy, but their avarice and ambition. They aimed at nothing less than the subjugation and plunder of the whole country. These powers were a portion of them landed, with implements and effects, and the remainder reserved on board their ships. They were met by the sons of liberty, both by sea and land, who were at length victorious, and this whole army were overcome, and their riches and armor, which was immense, were taken for spoil. This brilliant victory greatly enriched and strengthened the new empire of freedom, and at the same time nearly ruined the nations who commenced the war. They sued for peace, and finally obtained it on condition of perfect submission to the will of the conquerors. This gave them new and liberal laws and institutions, broke off the fetters of their old masters, and utterly forbade the use of arms or the art of war. These brilliant and highly commendable measures soon opened the eyes of millions more, and won them to the cause of liberty and truth. Other and distant nations, who had watched all these movements at length, saw the beauties of liberty and felt the force of truth, till finally, with one consent, they joined the same standard.

Thus, in one short century, the world is revolutionized; tyranny is dethroned; war has ceased forever; peace is triumphant, and truth and knowledge cover the earth."

Thus spake the Angel of the Prairies; and when he had ceased to speak, I still continued to listen; for such a blaze of glory and intelligence burst at once upon my view, and events so passing strange, so complicated, so unlooked for, had taken place in a single century, and had been related to me in so masterly a manner, that I stood overwhelmed with astonishment and wonder, and could hardly believe my senses. "Is it possible," thought I, "that a republic founded upon the most liberal principles, and established by the sweat and blood and tears of our renowned ancestors, and so cherished and respected by their children, has faded like the dazzling splendor of the morning's dawn? has withered like an untimely flower? and that, too, by the corruption of its own degenerate sons, the very persons who should have cherished it forever? Where was the spirit of patriotism, of freedom, of love of country which had once characterized the sons of liberty, and warmed the bosoms of Americans?"

With reflections like these I had commenced a lamentation over my fallen, lost and ruined country. But suddenly recollecting myself, and calling to mind the other events which had been related, my sorrow was turned into joy. I saw, although there had been great corruption and a general overthrow of our government and its institutions, yet many of the sons of noble sires had stood firm and unshaken in the cause of freedom; even amid the wreck of states and the crash of thrones, they had maintained their integrity, and when they had no longer a country or government to fight for, they retired to the plains of the West, carrying with them the pure spirit of freedom. There, in the midst of a more extensive, a richer and a better country, they had established a government more permanent, strong and lasting, and vastly more extensive and glorious, combining strength and solidity, with the most perfect liberty and freedom. Nor had their labors been confined to the narrow limits of their own immediate country and nation, but had burst the chains of tyranny and broken the yoke of bondage from the growing millions of all nations and colors; and where darkness, ignorance, superstition, cruelty and bloodshed had held dominion for ages, light had sprung up, truth had triumphed, and peace had commenced its universal reign. And where, a century ago, an extensive and fertile country lay desolate and lone, or partially occupied by ignorant and cruel savages, hundreds of millions of intelligent and happy beings were now enjoying all the sweets of domestic felicity. Why then, thought I, shall I mourn? The labors of our fathers were not in vain. On the contrary, the results have been a thousand times more glorious than their most sanguine expectations. The spirit of their institutions has been cherished and maintained. Their temple of liberty enlarged and perfected while the dross has been separated and destroyed, and the chaff blown to the four winds.

While these thoughts were passing in my mind, the Angel of the Prairies again called my attention. "Come," said he, " son of mortal, let us descend from this high eminence and enter the archives of the Temple of Freedom, and there you shall learn the secret springs, the fountain from which has emanated all this wisdom and greatness. You will then no longer wonder at the magnitude of this glorious organization, the perfection of its principles, or its unparalleled success." So, saying, we descended together through the same long and winding passage, till a door opened into a vast room in the second story of the building, which was gloriously finished and ornamented, and principally occupied with collections of antiquities and monuments and paintings, memorializing numerous and important events. Passing through in the midst of these, we entered a small room in which was carefully deposited numerous sacred books and records. From the midst of these the Angel of the Prairies selected a small volume entitled: "A true and perfect system of Civil and Religious Government, revealed from on High."

He then bade me be seated, gave me this book, and bade me read. So saying, he vanished from my sight. I opened the book and read the preface as, follows:

"There is a God in heaven who revealeth secrets. Wisdom and might are His. He changeth the times and the seasons. He removeth kings and setteth up kings. He giveth wisdom unto the wise and knowledge unto them that know understanding. His dominion is an everlasting dominion, and His kingdom is from generation to generation. He doth according to His will in the armies of heaven, and among the inhabitants of the earth. And none can stay His hand, or say unto Him, `What doeth thou?' All His works are truth, and His ways are judgment, and those that walk in pride He is able to abase. His kingdom is that which shall not be destroyed, and His dominion shall be even unto the end. As the Maker of the earth and the Father of the people, all power and authority of civil and religious government is vested in Him. He holds the prerogative of electing the officers and making the laws; He holds the right of reproving and admonishing the officers or of removing them at pleasure. Therefore all the forms of civil and religious government which are not appointed, organized and directed by divine revelation, are more or less imperfect and erroneous, and the administration thereof extremely liable to corruption and abuse. The only perfect system of government, then, is a Theocracy; that is, a government under the immediate, constant and direct superintendency of the Almighty. This order of government commenced in Eden, when God chose Adam for a ruler and gave him laws. It was perpetuated in his defendants, such as Seth, Enoch, Noah, Melchisedec, and so on, till it came down to Abraham, and was made hereditary in his seed forever. As it is written, `Kings shall be of thee, and princes shall come out of thy loins.'

"It was manifested clearly in Egypt--Pharaoh himself being instructed and governed by Joseph, as a revelator. Moses also delivered a nation from slavery, dethroned a tyrant, and governed in all things by these same principles. By these Joshua conquered, and by these the Judges of Israel ruled. By this authority Samuel reproved and displaced a corrupted priesthood, in the case of Eli and his sons. By it he annoints King Saul to reign in Israel, and by it he afterwards rejected him for transgression and anointed David in his stead. By virtue of this authority Elijah reproved and rejected Ahab and the priests of Baal, and then proceeded to anoint Jehu king and Elisha for prophet, and by this means remodeled the civil and religious administration of affairs, and saved a nation from the lowest depths of corruption and ruin. By this power, Daniel, the prophet, reproved and instructed Nebuchadnezzar, displaced Belteshazzar, and directed Cyrus; continually impressing upon kings and nations this one important principle, viz: 'That God is a revealer of secrets, and claims the right of government over kings and potentates of the earth." To convince Nebuchadnezzar of this one fact, he was driven out from his throne and from the society of men, to dwell among the beasts of the field and to eat grass as the ox, and afterwards restored to his kingdom again. And to convince all nations of this fact, King Nebuchadnezzar wrote his epistle to all nations and languages, in which he bore testimony to the same.

"By this authority Jesus Christ received all power in heaven and on earth, and was therefore seen by the prophet Daniel, coming in the clouds of heaven, to reign over all the earth. By this authority His Apostles governed those who would receive His kingdom in their day--being themselves chosen by the Lord, and not by the people. By this same authority the Gentile

Church and people would have been governed from that day to the present, without a schism or division of church or state, were it not for corruption and wickedness, which made war with the Saints, and overcame them, and changed times and laws, as was foretold by the prophet Daniel.

"By this authority the God of heaven promised, by all the holy prophets, that He would set up a kingdom that should destroy and break in pieces all these kingdoms, become universal, and stand forever. And that He would do this by the sitting of the Ancient of Days, whose raiment was white as snow, and whose hair was like the pure wool; while thousands of thousands ministered unto him, and ten thousand times ten thousand stood before him, and judgment was given to the Saints, and the time came that the Saints possessed the kingdom.

"By this authority the God of heaven has fulfilled that which He spoke by the mouths of His ancient prophets, by revealing from heaven and appointing and establishing a glorious kingdom which shall stand forever.

"Therefore sing, O Heavens!
And be joyful, O Earth!
For truth has triumphed;
Wisdom and knowledge rule;
Righteousness reigns;
And earth rests in lasting peace."

Thus ended the preface. I was about to read further, but was interrupted by the Angel of the Prairies. "Son of mortal," said he, "you have now read all you are permitted to read at the present time." So saying, he replaced the little book amid the archives of the temple, and bade me follow him. He then conducted me out of the temple, and said: "Son of mortal, you now understand the nature of the government have beheld. You see it is not a human monarchy, for man-made kings are tyrant. It is not an aristocracy, for in that case the few trample upon the rights of the many. It is not a democracy, for mobs composed of the mass, with no stronger power to check them, are the greatest tyrants and oppressors in the world. But it is a theocracy, where the great Eloheim, Jehovah, holds the superior honor. He selects the officers. He reveals and appoints the laws, and He counsels, reproves, directs, guides and holds the reins of government. The venerable Council which you beheld enthroned in majesty and clad in robes of white, with crowns upon their heads, is the order of the Ancient of Days, before whose august presence thrones have been cast down, and tyrants have ceased to rule. You have understood the secret purposes of Providence in relation to the prairies and the West, and of the earth and its destiny. Go forth on your journey, and wander no more; but tell the world of things to come."

At this I awoke, and behold, it was a dream. Instead of a glorious kingdom and city and temple, I beheld the morning sun shining through the crevices of the log cabin where I lodged. Instead of a century numbered with the past, I had spent a night of disturbed and unquiet slumber; and instead of the Angel of the Prairies standing by my side in the act of unfolding

"The secret purposes of fate,
Which govern men and guide the State,"
I beheld my landlord in the act of calling me to breakfast.

www.ingramcontent.com/pod-product-compliance
Lightning Source LLC
LaVergne TN
LVHW091322080426
835510LV00007B/608

9 7 8 1 6 3 1 1 8 5 4 1 0